THE PARABLES FOR TODAY

THE PARABLES FOR TODAY

Thomas Coates

CONCORDIA PUBLISHING HOUSE

ST. LOUIS   LONDON

By the same author:

THE CHAPEL HOUR
AUTHORITY IN THE CHURCH
THE PSALMS FOR TODAY
THE PROVERBS FOR TODAY
THE PROPHETS FOR TODAY
GOSPEL OF JOHN FOR TODAY

Concordia Publishing House, St. Louis, Missouri
Concordia Publishing House Ltd., London, E. C. 1
Copyright © 1971 Concordia Publishing House
Library of Congress Catalog Card No. 71-163071
ISBN 0-570-03011-0
MANUFACTURED IN THE UNITED STATES OF AMERICA

To
my colleagues, students, and friends
in Korea

PREFACE

The parables of Jesus are among the most familiar and best-loved portions of the New Testament. Rich in imagery, dramatic in style, their appeal lay in the fact that they spoke to the hearers in terms of their own experience and their own culture. In telling the parables Jesus showed Himself to be the Master Teacher.

The parables have never lost their relevance for the lives of God's people. Their appeal is timeless and universal. That is why the parables are truly "for today."

The parables, almost without exception, focus on one central truth: the kingdom of God—its nature, its expression, its goal. The parables are allegories about the Gospel of the kingdom.

Helmut Thielicke has compared the parables to a "coded telegram." The message is there, but we can understand it only if we know the code. That code is Christ.

Many books about the parables have been written. Dr. Thielicke and Bishop Gerald Kennedy have in recent years produced books of sermons based on the parables. Dr. Martin H. Scharlemann has written a concise and scholarly volume, *Proclaiming the Parables*, which makes detailed reference to the original Greek text.

The present volume is different in purpose and more modest in scope. It presents 21 meditations on the parables, in the hope that these may be helpful for private or family devotions, in school or college chapel exercises, and as devotional readings at meetings of church groups. It is the author's hope and prayer that these pages may bring to the user some measure of spiritual insight, strength, and consolation.

THOMAS COATES

Contents

THE PARABLES FOR TODAY

Love's Healing Power

But he, desiring to justify himself, said to Jesus, "And who is my neighbor?" Jesus replied, "A man was going down from Jerusalem to Jericho, and he fell among robbers, who stripped him and beat him, and departed, leaving him half dead. Now by chance a priest was going down that road; and when he saw him he passed by on the other side. So likewise a Levite, when he came to the place and saw him, passed by on the other side. But a Samaritan, as he journeyed, came to where he was; and when he saw him, he had compassion, and went to him and bound up his wounds, pouring on oil and wine; then he set him on his own beast and brought him to an inn, and took care of him. And the next day he took out two denarii and gave them to the innkeeper, saying, 'Take care of him; and whatever more you spend, I will repay you when I come back.' Which of these three, do you think, proved neighbor to the man who fell among the robbers?" He said, "The one who showed mercy on him." And Jesus said to him, "Go and do likewise." Luke 10:29-37

For its literary value alone this classic parable must find a place in any anthology of the world's great literature. The very title of its central character has become a household word, famous and familiar among people everywhere.

The parable is a favorite among all those who feel concern for the physical needs of their fellowmen. It crystallizes the spirit of charity, of social service, of humanitarianism. Small wonder that many hospitals bear the name "Good Samaritan"! To call a man a "Good Samaritan" is to pay him a high compliment indeed.

The importance of the parable, however, does not lie in its literary value, nor even in its humanitarian symbolism. We do not understand the parable aright unless we grasp its spiritual and theological meaning.

The spirit of the Good Samaritan is not just the spirit of St. Francis, or Florence Nightingale, or Albert Schweitzer, or the International Red Cross—all honor to them! Rather, it is the spirit of Christ. For the lesson of this parable is that "love is the fulfilling of the Law." And the source and motivation of such love is found alone in Christ.

Our Lord told this parable in answer to the lawyer's question, "Who is my neighbor?" The lawyer's premise, of course, was basically wrong. His question indicated an underlying, although unspoken, desire to avoid responsibility toward his fellowman. For love does not ask, "Who is my neighbor?" Rather, love asks, "Who needs me?" "Whom can I help?" "To whom can I show neighborly concern?"

There is a lesson to be learned, of course, from the examples of the priest and the Levite, who "passed by on the other side." Here were professional religionists who somehow failed to see the connection between religion and life, between doctrine and deeds, between orthodoxy and love. They may have been experts in theology, but they failed the basic theological test. They failed to love.

Love is not a theological abstraction. Love is concrete, practical, personal. Love concerns the neighbor. It concerns him because it sees in him the object of God's love.

Christ died for the neighbor. Can we not bind up his wounds?

Like most of the parables, this is basically a parable about God's kingdom. For membership in that kingdom the criterion is faith—faith in Christ and His atoning merits, faith in His free forgiveness, faith in the promises of His word.

But that faith must be active in love. Otherwise it is not genuine Christian faith at all. Faith, love, kingdom—they all belong together.

We had better not lose sight of this fact in our enthusiasm for this parable. Surely, let us build our hospitals, contribute to our charities, support our welfare programs. But let's not suppose that this alone makes us "Good Samaritans."

To be truly a "Good Samaritan" means to love Christ first, and to love our neighbor in Him. Such love is the Holy Spirit's work within us. And where that love exists, we shall not "pass by on the other side."

Where there is Christian love, there will be compassion, help, and healing for the bruised and helpless traveler along life's Jericho road.

Fair Wages

For the kingdom of heaven is like a householder who went out early in the morning to hire laborers for his vineyard. After agreeing with the laborers for a denarius a day, he sent them into his vineyard. And going out about the third hour he saw others standing idle in the marketplace; and to them he said, "You go into the vineyard too, and whatever is right I will give you." So they went. Going out again about the sixth hour and the ninth hour, he did the same. And about the eleventh hour he went out and found others standing; and he said to them, "Why do you stand here idle all day?" They said to him, "Because no one has hired us." He said to them, "You go into the vineyard too." And when evening came, the owner of the vineyard said to his steward, "Call the laborers and pay them their wages, beginning with the last, up to the first." And when those hired about the eleventh hour came, each of them received a denarius. Now when the first came, they thought they would receive more; but each of them also received a denarius. And on receiving it they grumbled at the householder, saying, "These last worked only one hour, and you have made them equal to us who have borne the burden of the day and the scorching heat." But he replied to one of them, "Friend, I am doing you no wrong; did you not agree with me for a denarius? Take what belongs to you, and go; I choose to give to this last as I give to you. Am I not allowed to do what I choose with what belongs to me? Or do you begrudge my generosity?" So the last will be first, and the first last. Matthew 20:1-16

Few issues in our day have aroused greater public concern than the relations between labor and management. Everyone is affected, either directly or indirectly — the workman who seeks higher pay; the union leaders who are ready to call a strike if their demands are not met; the employers who must try to reach an equitable agreement with their labor force; and the general public, "caught in the middle," that must ultimately pay the added costs of any wage increase.

In this context the economic policy expressed in this parable is wildly unrealistic. To pay the same wages for one hour's work as for 12 seems outrageously unfair. No workman today would stand for it. Union leaders would call a strike on the spot.

Even the laborers in the parable were incensed. They grumbled, "These last worked only one hour, and you have made them equal to us, who have borne the burden of the day and the scorching heat." They seemed to have an open-and-shut case.

Economically, yes. But our Lord did not tell this parable to establish an economic policy. His purpose was to drive home a spiritual lesson: We are saved by God's grace, not by our own works or merits.

There are no distinctions in God's plan of salvation between lifelong Christians and deathbed penitents. One thing they all have in common: the guilt of sin, the need of divine forgiveness. And that forgiveness is not dependent on length of service, or intensity of effort, or spiritual achievement. In God's kingdom there is no seniority system, no merit badge, no extra pay for overtime.

In that kingdom grace is the rule that prevails. No one can earn it. No one can enter without it. And no one dare question its "fairness."

"Am I not allowed to do what I choose with what belongs to me?" asked the householder in our parable. "Or do you begrudge my generosity?" Neither those who started early or those who came to work late could have labored at all if the master had not hired them. By the same token, God's grace alone calls men into His kingdom. They have no other claim on Him; they can only accept His mercy.

The meaning of this parable will be lost if anyone would infer from it that one might as well escape "the burden of the day and the scorching heat" by entering the Kingdom as late as possible, since in any case the "compensation" will be the same. For one thing, such an attitude in itself is an effective barrier to entering the kingdom at all.

But more: As difficult and strenuous as the Christian life may be, those who labor long in the vineyard will never have cause to regret it or to envy those who come in when the day is almost done. For "the burden of the day and the scorching heat" bring their own reward—growth in grace, a deep awareness of the unfailing help of God, strengthening of character, a truer sense of life's real and abiding values.

And while those who enter the Kingdom at the eleventh hour, as did the penitent thief on Calvary, are no less sure of the grace that has called them or the glory that awaits them, they have no cause to gloat over the burdens and trials they have missed. Rather, they will echo the poet's rueful words: "Alas, that I so late have known Thee!"

But—better late than never! The important thing is that they *have* come to know Him. And for all those whom God calls into His vineyard—at the first hour or at the eleventh—the divine promise holds true: "This is life eternal, that they may know Thee, the only true God, and Jesus Christ, whom Thou hast sent."

The Inner Force

Another parable He put before them, saying, "The kingdom of heaven is like a grain of mustard seed which a man took and sowed in his field; it is the smallest of all seeds, but when it has grown it is the greatest of shrubs and becomes a tree, so that the birds of the air come and make nests in its branches." He told them another parable. "The kingdom of heaven is like leaven which a woman took and hid in three measures of meal, till it was all leavened." Matthew 13:31-33

These are parables of external growth and of inner force. The comparisons which our Lord employs are striking and apt.

According to the first of these two parables the tiny mustard seed grows into a great and spreading tree, in whose branches the birds can make their nests. What kind of growth does Jesus have in mind in telling this parable? The application has often been made to the outward expansion and victorious power of the Christian church over the 2,000 years since its humble beginnings in Palestine.

History, however, does not fully support this explanation. For example, in Japan today — 400 years after the coming of the first Christian missionaries to the land — Christianity still numbers less than one percent of the population. In mainland China the once flourishing Christian community has been cruelly liquidated and driven underground. In Saudi Arabia there are more graves of Christian missionaries than there are professing Christians in that area today. On the basis of statistics, at least, there is little evidence that this parable is a guarantee of the church's numerical growth or of its organizational bigness.

We need to look deeper for the meaning of the mustard seed. The reference is not to external growth of the church as an organization, but to the spreading influence of the kingdom of heaven. And that kingdom, as our Lord says elsewhere, does not come "with observation." It is rather an inward, spiritual force. The "Kingdom" is actually Jesus' *kingship*, or reign, within the believer's heart.

In this sense, then, the kingdom indeed spreads like the proverbial mustard seed. First it permeates the Christian's own life. With Christ enshrined in his heart, he becomes a "new creature." He casts aside his old proud ambitions, his old selfish cravings, his old worldly habits. As he grows in grace, he embraces new and better values, new and purer loves, new and stronger convictions. The mustard seed is growing—within.

But the mustard seed is also growing without. For the Christian in whom the seed has been planted will inevitably "branch out" to influence others—his family, his associates, his community.

To underscore this lesson, our Lord immediately adds another illustration: the parable of the leaven. Here again the point of reference is to the "kingdom of heaven." Its influence is like that of yeast which the housewife puts into the dough. It is small and it is hidden, but it makes the bread rise and brings nourishment to the household.

God's kingdom in the human heart is like that—hidden but dynamic. True Christians are usually in the minority—in the business world, in politics, in the social group, on the campus. But when they allow God's ruling and indwelling Spirit to guide them in their words and actions, in their witness and example, they will be a wholesome leaven. And, lo and behold, things around them begin to change!

If the present trend toward moral laxity, disrespect of authority, and contempt for spiritual values is to be halted, and if a spiritual renewal is to begin, Christians must "leaven the lump" with the enlightening and ennobling Spirit of the Christ who lives and reigns within them.

No matter if the numbers are small, the resources few, the

prospects dim. Remember, the mustard seed is tiny. The leaven seems insignificant.

But look at the results!

Excuses

A man once gave a great banquet, and invited many; and at the time for the banquet he sent his servant to say to those who had been invited, "Come; for all is now ready." But they all alike began to make excuses. The first said to him, "I have bought a field, and I must go out and see it; I pray you, have me excused." And another said, "I have bought five yoke of oxen, and I go to examine them; I pray you, have me excused." And another said, "I have married a wife, and therefore I cannot come." So the servant came and reported this to his master. Then the householder in anger said to his servant, "Go out quickly to the streets and lanes of the city, and bring in the poor and maimed and blind and lame." And the servant said, "Sir, what you commanded has been done, and still there is room." And the master said to the servant, "Go out to the highways and hedges, and compel people to come in, that my house may be filled. For I tell you, none of those men who were invited shall taste my banquet." Luke 14:16-24

We usually find time to do the things that we really want to do. Somehow or other, schedules can be adjusted, appointments can be deferred, prior arrangements can be canceled to enable us to accept a coveted invitation, to meet a special friend, or to take advantage of some special opportunity that will bring us unexpected profit or pleasure.

The opposite is equally true. We can usually find excuses to avoid an unpleasant duty, to decline an unwanted invitation, or to bypass some event that would keep us from some more desirable activity. Sometimes to our relief we can offer excuses that are genuinely valid. Too often, alas, we resort to alibis that are no better than thinly disguised fabrications.

The three men in our parable offered excuses that were apparently valid. They were genuinely busy—two with newly acquired property, the other with a newly acquired wife. They sincerely felt that they could not spare the time to accept the banquet invitation that the servant had brought them. On the face of it, their attitude might even seem commendable. The first two put business before pleasure, while the third preferred to spend time with his bride rather than to leave her, even temporarily, for an outside social engagement.

And yet the host was angry when he heard these excuses. His hospitality had been spurned. His pride had been wounded. It was obvious that the invited guests did not prize his invitation very highly.

Like most other parables which He told, our Lord used this story to drive home some sharp lessons concerning the kingdom — what it is and how men react to it.

It is quite clear from the parable that a great many people are reluctant to accept the Lord's invitation. Excuses, excuses — there seems to be no limit to either their variety or their inge- nuity. "I have to keep my store open on Sunday." "Sunday is the only day I can sleep late." "I must stay home to prepare dinner for the family." "There are too many hypocrites in the church." "I don't have good enough clothes to wear to church." "I don't like the minister." "The church is too 'cath'lick.'" "I had too much church when I was a child." "Church people are too 'stuffy.'"

And then there are some distinctly modern versions: "The church is not relevant." "The church doesn't communicate with youth." "The Ten Commandments are out of date." "We don't want sermons — we want action!" "The church has nothing to say in a scientific age like this." "The church won't let me 'do my thing.'" But why go on? The list is almost endless.

No doubt many of these excuses are offered sincerely. There is obviously at least some truth in certain of these objections. Doubtless there are some genuine conflicts that people find hard to overcome. And yet the Lord, like the householder in the parable, grows angry when His invitation is refused.

Why were the excuses in the parable rejected? There is nothing wrong—Karl Marx and his modern disciples notwithstanding—in owning a field, whether in Palestine or in California, or in buying a yoke of oxen, whether in Palestine or in Korea. And there is certainly nothing wrong in marrying a wife, whether in the first century or the twentieth. The activities of the three men in the parable were quite legitimate.

The problem was the matter of priorities. Is it more important to buy a piece of property than to accept the Gospel invitation? Is it more important to examine five yoke of oxen—or a new Volkswagen—than to go to church? Is it more important to spend time with your wife—even a new one—than to hear God's Word?

The fault of these three men—and of all the legion of their modern counterparts—lay in their wrong priorities. They put property, profit, pleasure ahead of God, His Word, His kingdom. And so the Master's decree is that "none of those men who were invited shall taste of my banquet." They showed a false sense of priorities.

But the banquet table will not be empty. From the highways and hedges, from the streets and lanes of the city other guests will come to the feast in surging throngs. These are "the poor and maimed and blind and lame"—those who have no strength in themselves and who seek respite from the ills and troubles of life.

The Gospel invitation goes out to all. Those who accept the Master's summons are the ones who feel their need, who rue their sins, who seek His grace, who long to be fed at His table.

And at the heavenly banquet there is room enough for all.

Unequal Gifts, Equal Grace

For it will be as when a man going on a journey called his servants and entrusted to them his property; to one he gave five talents*, to another two, to another one, to each according to his ability. Then he went away. He who had received the five talents went at once and traded with them; and he made five talents more. So also, he who had the two talents made two talents more. But he who had received the one talent went and dug in the ground and hid his master's money. Now after a long time the master of those servants came and settled accounts with them. And he who had received the five talents came forward, bringing five talents more, saying, "Master, you delivered to me five talents; here I have made five talents more." His master said to him, "Well done, good and faithful servant; you have been faithful over a little, I will set you over much; enter into the joy of your master." And he also who had the two talents came forward, saying, "Master, you delivered to me two talents; here I have made two talents more." His master said to him, "Well done, good and faithful servant; you have been faithful over a little, I will set you over much; enter into the joy of your master." He also who had received the one talent came forward, saying, "Master, I knew you to be a hard man, reaping where you did not sow, and gathering where you did not winnow; so I was afraid, and I went and hid your talent in the ground. Here you have what is yours." But his master answered him, "You wicked and slothful servant! You knew that I reap where I have not sowed, and gather where I have not winnowed? Then you ought to have invested my money with the bankers, and at my coming I should have received what was my own with interest. So take the talent from him, and give it to him who has the ten talents. For to everyone who has will more be given, and he will have

*The talent was a monetary unit in Biblical times, perhaps equaling about 1,000 dollars.

abundance; but from him who has not, even what he has will be taken away. And cast the worthless servant into the outer darkness; there men will weep and gnash their teeth." Matthew 25:14-30

"Equality" is one of the most popular themes of our time. Equality of rights, of opportunity, of status, of income — these are some of the aspects of the subject currently being debated with varying degrees of intensity, in our own country and in other parts of the world.

Equality, however, is a complex term. There can be no question of the spiritual equality of all men in the sight of God. All men are equally the objects of God's judgment upon sin. But all men are also equally the objects of God's saving grace through Christ. In His kingdom "there is neither Jew nor Greek, there is neither slave nor free, there is neither male nor female; for you are all one in Christ Jesus," declares St. Paul. This is true spiritual equality — the kind of equality that has real and eternal value.

There should be no argument, either, that in civil affairs there should be equality of justice for all citizens; equality of opportunity to participate in the political process, to receive an education, and to enjoy the protection of the law. Inequality and discrimination in these matters are offenses against both civic righteousness and the Christian ideal.

In another respect, however, inequality is an inescapable fact of life. All men simply do not have the same mental endowments, the same physical strength, the same social advantages. The factors of both heredity and environment make it inevitable that there will always be economic, social, and intellectual differences among men.

The well-known parable of the talents offers an interesting study in the polarity between equality and inequality. In the economic sense the three men in the parable were obviously unequal. One had received five talents, another two, and another only one. The distribution, indeed, was made "to each

26

according to his ability," so that in this respect, too, they were unequal.

In a spiritual sense, however, they were equal. To each of them the master had given equal responsibility, in proportion to the amount which he had entrusted to them. It was their obligation to invest his money wisely, that they might show a profit upon his return.

The first two were faithful to their trust. Each of them had doubled his investment during the master's absence. Small wonder that he commended them highly and gave them commensurate rewards!

The case of the third servant, however, was quite different. To be sure, he had not squandered or misappropriated the one talent entrusted to him. Quite the contrary. To be perfectly safe, he had dug a hole and hidden the talent in the ground, to keep it secure until the master's return.

Far from commending him, however, the master berated the servant and called him "wicked and slothful." The charge against him was not dishonesty but lack of courage, zeal, faithfulness. In a word, the third servant had been a poor steward. The master did not condemn him for failing to bring a return of five talents, but for failing to make even a one-talent profit.

The lesson is obvious. Some of us are five-talent, some two-talent individuals. Others of us must get along with only one talent. But there is no such thing as a no-talent person!

What God expects of us is a fair return on His investment in us, in just proportion to the nature and extent of our gifts. He will not fault the one-talent man for not bringing in a five-talent profit. But He will be angry indeed with the five-talent man for producing on only a one- or two- or even four-talent basis.

It is all a question of stewardship. God does not expect every preacher to be a St. Paul, or every doctor to be a

Schweitzer, or every mother to be a Monica, or every teacher to be a Montessori, or every business man to be a Rockefeller, or every soldier to be a MacArthur, or every athlete to be a Jesse Owens.

What God does expect of every one of His people is faithfulness, diligence, zeal in the use of his talents, whether they be five or two or only one. And the motivation should not be selfish ambition, pride, or greed, but better service and the greater glory of God.

Unequal we may be in the number and quality of our talents. But equal we all are in our relationship to God—equally dependent on Him, equally responsible to Him, equally indebted to Him for all His gifts and graces.

And for God's faithful servants, no matter how many or how few their talents, there is the sure prospect of the perfect equality of heaven.

A Story of Rejection

And He began to tell the people this parable: "A man planted a vineyard, and let it out to tenants, and went into another country for a long while. When the time came, he sent a servant to the tenants, that they should give him some of the fruit of the vineyard; but the tenants beat him and sent him away empty-handed. And he sent another servant; him also they beat and treated shamefully, and sent him away empty-handed. And he sent yet a third; this one they wounded and cast out. Then the owner of the vineyard said, 'What shall I do? I will send my beloved son; it may be they will respect him.' But when the tenants saw him, they said to themselves, 'This is the heir; let us kill him, that the inheritance may be ours.' And they cast him out of the vineyard and killed him. What then will the owner of the vineyard do to them? He will come and destroy those tenants, and give the vineyard to others." When they heard this, they said, "God forbid!" But He looked at them and said, "What then is this that is written: 'The very Stone which the builders rejected has become the Head of the corner'? Every one who falls on that Stone will be broken to pieces; but when it falls on anyone it will crush him." Luke 20:9—18

The lesson of this parable—recorded three times in the Gospels—is quite obvious. Even the scribes and the chief priests got the point, for St. Luke goes on to say that "they perceived that He had told this parable against them."

The parable is a transparent reference to the incredible love and patience of God in sending prophet after prophet to His chosen people to prepare them for the coming Messiah and to incite them to faith and obedience. In varying ways the prophets were reviled, rejected, even killed.

Finally the Master sent His "beloved Son," who suffered the crowning indignity, the ultimate rejection. He was slain by those whom He had come to save.

In the parable the slaying of the heir finally — and understandably — exhausted the owner's patience. "He will come and destroy those tenants, and give the vineyard to others."

It would be a mistake to concentrate on the details of this parable. They simply serve as the framework to convey a profound spiritual lesson. It would be a still greater mistake, however, to use this parable as an excuse for a condemnation of the Jewish people.

The parable is not simply about the Jews. It is also about us. Its relevance is universal and timeless. The wicked vinedressers still exist today. God's prophets are still being rejected. God's Son is still, in effect, being crucified.

The modern vineyardists, of course, are usually more subtle and sophisticated. Stones and spears and faggots are the relics of a cruder age. But unbelief, spiritual pride, and secularism are no less deadly for all their veneer of respectability.

Nowadays the grossest heresy, the most blatant unbelief, the most callous blasphemy often appear in the guise of "modernity," "enlightened liberalism," and "relevance." Increasingly they flourish in prestigious pulpits, in well-endowed divinity schools, and in the influential editorial columns of church publications.

The church's evangelistic task is being supplanted by social and political activism. Many preachers are more concerned about foreign policy than about theology. The unchangeable canons of Christian morality are giving way to moral relativism. Ethical absolutes are yielding to the new permissiveness. Even in church bodies with a long history of staunch conservatism, tolerance is being expressed for extramarital sex, for militant disobedience, and for concessions to the fads and gimmicks of our secularistic age.

But unbelief — crude or subtle, open or concealed — will meet its inevitable doom. The world and all it represents: "the lust of the flesh, the lust of the eyes, the pride of life" will pass away. For although Christ is "the Stone which the builders rejected," time will prove that "everyone who falls on that Stone will be broken to pieces, but when it falls on anyone it will crush him."

For Christ Himself remains eternally the Cornerstone — of the Gospel, of His Church, of our lives.

Rich Man, Poor Man

There was a rich man, who was clothed in purple and fine linen and who feasted sumptuously every day. And at his gate lay a poor man named Lazarus, full of sores, who desired to be fed with what fell from the rich man's table; moreover the dogs came and licked his sores. The poor man died and was carried by the angels to Abraham's bosom. The rich man also died and was buried; and in Hades, being in torment, he lifted up his eyes, and saw Abraham far off and Lazarus in his bosom. And he called out, "Father Abraham, have mercy upon me, and send Lazarus to dip the end of his finger in water and cool my tongue; for I am in anguish in this flame." But Abraham said, "Son, remember that you in your lifetime received your good things, and Lazarus in like manner evil things; but now he is comforted here, and you are in anguish. And besides all this, between us and you a great chasm has been fixed, in order that those who would pass from here to you may not be able, and none may cross from there to us." And he said, "Then I beg you, father, to send him to my father's house, for I have five brothers, so that he may warn them, lest they also come into this place of torment." But Abraham said, "They have Moses and the prophets; let them hear them." And he said, "No, father Abraham; but if someone goes to them from the dead, they will repent." He said to him, "If they do not hear Moses and the prophets, neither will they be convinced if some one should rise from the dead." Luke 16:19-31

There is a difference of opinion among Bible scholars as to whether or not this story is actually a parable. We are not here concerned about the technicalities of this definition. What we are interested in is the vital lesson that this story so vividly conveys.

The account of the rich man (whom tradition has called Dives) and poor Lazarus is one of the most familiar in the Bible.

It is, however, frequently misunderstood and misapplied. It should be obvious that the point of the story is not that those who are rich are automatically doomed to perdition, and that they will get their just deserts in the hereafter. It is just as foolish to infer that poverty in this life is a sure guarantee of heaven.

It is not a sin to be rich. It is a sin to misuse one's riches. And obviously, material wealth involves many temptations that are unknown to the person with a modest bank account, or with none at all.

On the other hand, it is not a virtue in itself to be poor. Sometimes a person is to blame for his own poverty. More often a man's poverty is due to circumstances beyond his control. Untold millions live in dire need because of the economic and social injustice that blights so much of contemporary life in every country in the world.

Sometimes lack of this world's goods increases a man's dependence on God and his hope of better things to come. But it is equally true, as Solomon sagely observed, that poverty may drive a man to curse his fate and to steal from his fellowman.

The rich man in Hades was in torment. The anguish that he felt was not only physical but also mental and spiritual. The "flames" are largely symbolical of the true nature of hell—eternal, conscious separation from the presence of God. And his anguish was intensified by the realization that the beggar whom he had despised in this life was now in heaven, enjoying the peace and security of "Abraham's bosom." The chasm between them was so wide and so unbridgeable that Lararus could not cross over to slake the rich man's burning thirst with so much as a drop of cooling water.

Even though his own destiny was sealed, Dives still clung to the hope that his five surviving brothers might be spared the hideous fate that had befallen him. The wild notion occurred to him that if Lazarus might return to earth to warn them, they might be shocked into repentance.

But when Dives appealed for Lazarus to return from the dead to confront his brothers, the answer from above was firm and clear: "They have Moses and the prophets; let them hear them." If men refuse to hear the Biblical witness, no apparition from the grave will convince them.

Men have always been fascinated by the occult. Ever since the witch of Endor conjured up the ghost of Samuel, men have sought to communicate with the dead, to peer into the mysteries of the unknown beyond. The cult of the soothsayers, who claim the power of contact with departed spirits, has many adherents. Unscrupulous mediums prey upon the fears and griefs and hopes of gullible and superstitious people. In recent times wide publicity was given to the efforts of a prominent American churchman, bereaved by his son's suicide, to converse with the young man in the other world.

God does not effect a man's conversion by performing a special miracle for his benefit. He will not grant a supernatural vision to persuade a man to repent.

The key word in the story of the rich man and Lazarus is *hear*. The way to salvation is to hear and receive God's Word with a believing heart. The Word alone is the means to eternal life.

Moses and the prophets have had their day. Their mission was to proclaim and to prepare the way for the coming Messiah. Now He has come in the person of Jesus Christ, the Word made flesh. He lived, suffered, died for man's redemption. And after death He reappeared, not as a ghostly apparition but as the resurrected Lord.

To hear Him, to believe Him, is to live—now and forever.

Piety, Pride, and Pardon

He also told this parable to some who trusted in themselves that they were righteous and despised others: "Two men went up into the temple to pray, one a Pharisee and the other a tax collector. The Pharisee stood and prayed thus with himself, 'God, I thank Thee that I am not like other men, extortioners, unjust, adulterers, or even like this tax collector. I fast twice a week, I give tithes of all that I get.' But the tax collector, standing far off, would not even lift up his eyes to heaven, but beat his breast, saying, 'God, be merciful to me a sinner!' I tell you, this man went down to his house justified rather than the other; for every one who exalts himself will be humbled, but he who humbles himself will be exalted." Luke 18:9-14

We have no difficulty in identifying the villain and the hero in this familiar parable. The proud Pharisee has become the proverbial symbol of arrogant self-righteousness. The despised tax collector, or publican, is the epitome of penitent humility. There is truth in this identification, of course.

We need, however, to look somewhat more deeply into the meaning of this parable. The Pharisee was a solid citizen. He was honest in his business dealings. His family life was beyond reproach. His employees found him just and fair. He was a faithful churchgoer. He was generous, even sacrificial, in his giving. He was abstemious in his personal habits.

No one would question the high moral standards, the stellar character, of this man. He would be an asset to any community, any church.

We cannot even blame him for being thankful that he was not a swindler or racketeer, like some other people he could mention. Is it wrong for us to be glad that we are not gangsters, or wifebeaters, or dope peddlers? Isn't it quite natural for us to be happy that we were not born Al Capone, or Adolf Hitler, or

Lee Harvey Oswald? We have real cause to be thankful that we have been spared from that kind of fate.

The Pharisee's fatal mistake, however, was in his standard of comparison. Naturally a comparison between himself and a grafter or extortioner made him look good. But a more honest comparison would have been with the high and holy standards that God Himself has set—for the Pharisee and for everyone else.

Measured by that yardstick, the Pharisee should have realized that he had miserably failed—as have we all. For "we have all sinned and come short of the glory of God," and "there is none righteous, there is none that doeth good, no, not one."

The Pharisee's besetting sin was pride. And pride, indeed, is the root sin. For pride is actually a form of idolatry—the idolatry of self. And that is the worst idolatry of all.

There is something of the Pharisee in all of us. For we are all by nature proud, selfish, vain. And when pride takes root in our heart, we shunt God into the background, demean His grace, misuse His gifts. Before we point the finger of scorn at the Pharisee, we had better look into the mirror.

And what about the tax collector? Ah, there's the example for us to follow! But why? Not because there is any special virtue in being a "publican," certainly. In fact, we can be quite glad that we are not "publicans" as the New Testament describes them.

Actually, however, we are all "publicans" in our own way. None of us has any more right to lift up his eyes to heaven than did the publican in the temple.

His particular virtue, however, lay in his *repentance*. It was not just a show of humility, for excessive humility is actually an inverse kind of pride. It was rather a genuine remorse that caused him to beat his breast and cry, "God, be merciful to me, a sinner!" With remorse went trust in God's sure mercy and forgiveness, full and free.

Such remorse must be ours, too, for our claims to virtue are no better than the publican's. Then mercy, too, will be ours. And then, too, we shall "go down to our house justified"—by God's grace, for the sake of Christ.

For the divine rule prevails: "Every one who exalts himself will be humbled, but he who humbles himself will be exalted."

Rootless Religion

And when a great crowd came together and people from town after town came to Him, He said in a parable: "A sower went out to sow his seed; and as he sowed, some fell along the path, and was trodden under foot, and the birds of the air devoured it. And some fell on the rock; and as it grew up, it withered away, because it had no moisture. And some fell among thorns; and the thorns grew with it and choked it. And some fell into good soil and grew, and yielded a hundredfold." As He said this, He called out, "He who has ears to hear, let him hear." And when His disciples asked Him what this parable meant, He said, "To you it has been given to know the secrets of the kingdom of God; but for others they are in parables, so that seeing they may not see, and hearing they may not understand. Now the parable is this: The seed is the Word of God. The ones along the path are those who have heard; then the devil comes and takes away the Word from their hearts, that they may not believe and be saved. And the ones on the rock are those who, when they hear the Word, receive it with joy; but these have no root, they believe for a while and in time of temptation fall away. And as for what fell among the thorns, they are those who hear, but as they go on their way they are choked by the cares and riches and pleasures of life, and their fruit does not mature. And as for that in the good soil, they are those who, hearing the Word, hold it fast in an honest and good heart, and bring forth fruit with patience." Luke 8:4-15

Jesus was a master teacher because He spoke to the people in terms of their own experience. This parable offers a good example of His technique. Palestine was an agricultural country. Everyone knew about soil and seed and sowing. Jesus met His hearers on common ground, therefore, when He told them the parable of the four kinds of soil.

This parable is unique, however, in that Jesus clearly

explained the spiritual meaning of the story. One need not be a farmer—and in our urbanized society their number is decreasing—to know exactly what Jesus had in mind when He told this parable.

A sower goes out, scattering his seed right and left with cheerful abandon. Some drops on the roadway, where it is quickly trodden underfoot and where the birds consume it.

The seed, says Jesus, is the Word of God. It is sown far and wide—particularly in our own day, when the airwaves carry the Gospel to every nook and corner of the world and when the Word in written form has been translated into every major language and dialect. There is literally "no speech or language where its voice is not heard."

There is no dearth of hearers, indeed. The tragedy, however, is that too many are like the hard and arid pathway. For these the Word "goes in one ear and out the other." Like the birds who devoured the seed, the devil quickly moves into their hearts before the Word has a chance to take root. Their time of grace is real but brief.

Other seed, according to our Lord, falls on the rocky ground. It begins to grow, to be sure, but without moisture it soon withers away. "The ones on the rock," Jesus explains, "are those who, when they hear the Word, receive it with joy."

We all know people like that. A rousing sermon, an emotional hymn, a fervent call to repentance, and suddenly they "get religion." But when the surge of emotion subsides and the hard realities of life press in upon them, their religion "peters out." As our Lord puts it: "These have no root; they believe for a while and in time of temptation fall away."

Religion is more than a passing emotion. Faith needs more than mood or atmosphere to sustain it. Like the seed, faith needs constant moisture—the spiritual nourishment that comes from a steady exposure to the Word.

The third kind of soil proves equally inhospitable to the

seed from the sower's hand. "Some fell among thorns," Jesus declares, "and the thorns grew with it and choked it." These are the hearers of the Word who are "choked by the cares and riches and pleasure of this life, and their fruit does not mature."

It is a rule of nature that if a seed is to bear fruit, it must first "die." But these hearers are not willing to "die" to sin, to sacrifice "all the vain things that charm us most." They want to cling to their old loves, their old follies, their old cares. Before long these will choke their newfound faith. The thorns don't give the seed a chance to grow.

Happily, the parable ends on an optimistic note. The seed that falls on good soil takes root and yields abundant fruit. This is the sure result when the Word is "held fast" in "an honest and good heart"—one that is open to the benign influence of the Spirit and that awaits His promises "with patience."

In the deepest sense, we understand and apply this parable aright when we realize that within each of us there exist these four kinds of soil. We too are tempted to be shallow, to grow hardened, to allow life's thorns to choke our spirit. The good soil needs constantly to be cultivated. And for this we need the continuing influence of God's Word and the power of His fructifying Spirit.

"He who has ears to hear, let him hear."

Prayer Power

And He said to them, "Which of you who has a friend will go to him at midnight and say to him, 'Friend, lend me three loaves; for a friend of mine has arrived on a journey, and I have nothing to set before him'; and he will answer from within, 'Do not bother me; the door is now shut, and my children are with me in bed; I cannot get up and give you anything'? I tell you, though he will not get up and give him anything because he is his friend, yet because of his importunity he will rise and give him whatever he needs. And I tell you, Ask, and it will be given you; seek, and you will find; knock, and it will be opened to you. For every one who asks receives, and he who seeks finds, and to him who knocks it will be opened." Luke 11:5-10

And He told them a parable, to the effect that they ought always to pray and not lose heart. He said, "In a certain city there was a judge who neither feared God nor regarded man; and there was a widow in that city who kept coming to him and saying, 'Vindicate me against my adversary.' For a while he refused; but afterward he said to himself, 'Though I neither fear God nor regard man, yet because this widow bothers me, I will vindicate her, or she will wear me out by her continual coming.'" And the Lord said, "Hear what the unrighteous judge says. And will not God vindicate His elect, who cry to Him day and night? Will He delay long over them? I tell you, He will vindicate them speedily." Luke 18:1-8

"Never give up!" is the simple but powerful lesson that summarizes both these parables. Persistence is a virtue that usually "pays off" in the end. This is true in human relations. It is supremely true in the relationship of man to God that finds expression in prayer.

The reluctant friend and the unjust judge were not exemplary persons. The one was selfish—too selfish to inconvenience himself in order to accommodate his friend in a time of special emergency. The other was cynical and callous, openly boasting that he "neither feared God or regarded man." He was even unwilling to give a poor widow the justice that she sought.

Both men, however, despite their natural inclinations, finally yielded under the persistent pressure that was applied to them. The selfish householder, growing tired of the insistent clamoring and pounding of his friend, got up and gave him the bread he needed. The godless judge, wearied by the unrelenting pressure of the aggrieved widow, decided that the best way to be rid of her was to yield to her demands.

In both cases the motivation was something less than noble. The point that Jesus wants to make, however, is clear: Persistence brings results.

Our Lord told these parables to underscore the importance of persistent prayer. The lesson is obvious: If even weak, ignoble men with selfish motivation will reward persistent effort, how much more will the just and holy God, whose only motive is love, respond to the insistent pleas and the crying needs of His own beloved children?

But more: In these parables our Lord makes clear the true nature of prayer. In the words of Bishop Gerald Kennedy, too many people regard prayer as "an emergency action of short duration." In a time of crisis—exposure to physical danger, a crucial family problem, a period of painful illness—men quickly turn to God in prayer. But when the emergency is over and the situation returns to normal, men just as quickly forget about Him and resume their self-centered, prayerless way of life. They use God only on a "standby" basis. For them prayer is like the oxygen mask over an airplane seat. It is useful in an emergency, but they would not think of using it habitually.

For the Christian, however, prayer should be a way of life. That is what St. Paul means when he bids us to "pray without ceasing." We should live in the constant awareness of God's presence and of His unfailing love and care for us in all our needs. Persistence in prayer actually means that the channel of communication between God and ourselves is always kept open.

If that is the case, we shall not wait for a special occasion or a special place for our prayers. Not only in church but also on the street, in the shop, on the playing field, in the kitchen, in the schoolroom — that is to say, in the midst of the daily routine, amid the normal activities and experiences of life — we need to be in touch with God through prayer.

This is the true meaning of persistent prayer. And when prayer is indeed our "way of life," we shall experience the fulfillment of the divine promise, "Ask, and it will be given you; seek, and you will find; knock, and it will be opened to you."

Individual Worth

So He told them this parable: "What man of you, having a hundred sheep, if he has lost one of them, does not leave the ninety-nine in the wilderness, and go after the one which is lost, until he finds it? And when he has found it, he lays it on his shoulders, rejoicing. And when he comes home, he calls together his friends and his neighbors, saying to them, 'Rejoice with me, for I have found my sheep which was lost.' Even so, I tell you, there will be more joy in heaven over one sinner who repents than over ninety-nine righteous persons who need no repentance. Or what woman, having ten silver coins, if she loses one coin, does not light a lamp and sweep the house and seek diligently until she finds it? And when she has found it, she calls together her friends and neighbors, saying, 'Rejoice with me, for I have found the coin which I had lost.' Just so, I tell you, there is joy before the angels of God over one sinner who repents." Luke 15:3-10

It is a mark of a civilized society—and not necessarily a "Christian" one, for that matter—that it places supreme value upon an individual life. A child who has fallen into a deep well, a sailor adrift on the sea, an injured mountain climber clinging precariously to a remote ledge—cases such as these have brought forth great and heartwarming demonstrations of human concern, the outpouring of large sums of money, countless hours of voluntary assistance, strenuous and even sacrificial efforts on the part of public and private agencies, and of individuals as well. All this is done in the interest of saving a single human life.

As noble and as generous as these expressions of human concern may be, they pale into insignificance when compared with our Lord's concern for the well-being of a single human soul. That is the point of the two "parables of the lost" which

44

Jesus told in refuting the carping criticism of the scribes and Pharisees over His friendliness with "sinners." Why, He even ate with them!

The parable of the lost sheep is especially well known. It is the theme of one of the most stirring pieces of English hymnody, "The Ninety and Nine." It has inspired many works of art, of which perhaps the best shows our Lord leaning precariously over a cliff, His arm reaching down to grasp the lamb that had become lodged in a thicket, far above the yawning abyss.

The lesson is clear: If even a human shepherd will leave the rest of the flock behind in his effort to find the one lost sheep—disregarding all the hardships and dangers of the search—how much more will the Lord expend every effort, even at the cost of His own divine life, to recall and reclaim the lost and wayward sinner! No matter that the "sheep" has gone astray through his own folly and neglect—the Lord's search for him is no less intense, and His joy over the safe return to the fold is all the greater.

The same divine concern for the erring sinner is illustrated by the parable of the lost coin. The frugal housewife, dismayed over the loss of even one coin out of the ten which she had laid aside to pay her household bills, will literally turn the house upside down in her frantic effort to find the missing money. And when at last she has found it, she will joyfully tell the whole neighborhood about it.

The individual *does* count with God. No matter how mean and selfish, how unlovely and unlovable, how dissolute and depraved he may be, God is not willing to give him up for lost. Our Lord is never ready to "write off" anyone—not even the most "hopeless" case.

This is not merely a pious theory, a pleasant fiction. God proved it in the most dramatic way. He yielded His own Son to bitter suffering and cruel death, so that every "lost sheep"

45

might be found, every "lost coin" reclaimed.

His people can do no less—no less than share our Lord's concern for the wayward, the erring, the lost. These abound in our midst—the alcoholic, the drug addict, the "seeker after lust," the gambler, the moneygrubber, and the vast legion of "decent godless people" who live only for clothes and cars, fun and food and football—all of which may be good in themselves, but which they allow to obscure the highest Good.

All of these people without God—from skid row to suburbia —are infinitely valuable in God's sight. The premium that He placed on their redemption was the sacrifice of His own Son.

And when even one of these returns to the fold, there is joy among God's angels, and the heavens resound with song.

How Firm a Foundation!

Everyone then who hears these words of Mine and does them will be like a wise man who built his house upon the rock; and the rain fell, and the floods came, and the winds blew and beat upon that house, but it did not fall, because it had been founded on the rock. And everyone who hears these words of Mine and does not do them will be like a foolish man who built his house upon the sand; and the rains fell, and the floods came, and the winds blew and beat against that house, and it fell; and great was the fall of it. Matthew 7:24-27

This parable illustrates a very simple truth, but one that is too often and too easily forgotten. A firm foundation is important—in building a house, in building a life.

It is significant that Jesus told the parable of the house upon the rock at the conclusion of His Sermon on the Mount. Recalling the profound lessons in Christian living that He had just given to His listeners, He cites "these words of Mine" as the sure foundation upon which to build an unshakable faith, an unyielding hope, a secure life.

A hillside house can slide from its foundation after a heavy rain. Such a house is usually damaged beyond repair. The fault obviously lay in the weakness of its foundation. The architect, the builder, the owner—all had taken a foolish and needless risk, like the foolish man in the parable who "built his house upon the sand."

Many people build their lives upon a foundation of sand. Reliance on one's own strength of mind or body, on financial resources, on family or social "connections" is a flimsy basis on which to build a life or to plan for the future. When the winds of trouble blow, and when the floods of adversity beat against a foundation like that, it is bound to crumble. To build a life upon the sand is to invite sure disaster.

We cannot keep the gale from howling, or the rain from falling, or the waters from flooding. Trouble, sorrow, sickness, reversal, pain — these are the common lot of man. We can, however, keep them from destroying the foundation on which our life is built.

That means, of course, that we must choose a sure and firm foundation on which to build. Our Lord shows what that foundation must be: "These words of Mine" — His words of pardon and peace, of hope and strength, of light and life. Those words of His are not merely written in a book. Through the Spirit's power they are infused into our lives.

Jesus stresses the fact that to build upon the rock means not only to *hear* His words but to *do* them. Hearing God's words is quite easy; it takes little effort. But doing those words is another matter altogether. It not only requires special effort; it demands life commitment.

To *do* His words means to believe in them implicitly — as our guide through life, as our surety for heaven. But to *do* His words also means to translate them into action — into love for our fellowman, into the service of all that is right and just and true. "Be doers of the Word, and not hearers only, deceiving your own selves," warns St. James.

The Christian life means "faith active in love." Such a life is built upon the rock.

> *How firm a foundation, ye saints of the Lord,*
> *Is laid for your faith in His excellent Word!*

Back from the Far Country

And He said, "There was a man who had two sons; and the younger of them said to his father, 'Father, give me the share of property that falls to me.' And he divided his living between them. Not many days later, the younger son gathered all he had and took his journey into a far country, and there he squandered his property in loose living. And when he had spent everything, a great famine arose in that country, and he began to be in want. So he went and joined himself to one of the citizens of that country, who sent him into his fields to feed swine. And he would gladly have fed on the pods that the swine ate; and no one gave him anything. But when he came to himself he said, 'How many of my father's hired servants have bread enough and to spare, but I perish here with hunger! I will arise and go to my father, and I will say to him, "Father, I have sinned against heaven and before you; I am no longer worthy to be called your son; treat me as one of your hired servants."' And he arose and came to his father. But while he was yet at a distance, his father saw him and had compassion, and ran and embraced him and kissed him. And the son said to him, 'Father, I have sinned against heaven and before you; I am no longer worthy to be called your son.' But the father said to his servants, 'Bring quickly the best robe, and put it on him; and put a ring on his hand, and shoes on his feet; and bring the fatted calf and kill it, and let us eat and make merry; for this my son was dead, and is alive again; he was lost, and is found.' And they began to make merry.

"Now his elder son was in the field; and as he came and drew near to the house, he heard music and dancing. And he called one of the servants and asked what this meant. And he said to him, 'Your brother has come, and your father has killed the fatted calf, because he has received him safe and sound.' But he was angry and refused to go in. His father came out and entreated him, but he answered his father, 'Lo, these many years I have served you, and I never disobeyed your *command; yet you never game me a kid, that I might make merry with my friends. But when this son of yours came, who has devoured your living with harlots, you killed for him the fatted calf!' And he said to him, 'Son, you are always with me, and all that is mine is yours. It was fitting to make merry and be glad, for this your brother was dead, and is alive; he was lost, and is found.'"* Luke 15:11-24

This parable, so familiar, so oft retold, abounds with so many absorbing details, such rich imagery, that a whole series of sermons might well be preached on it. The central lesson, however, is actually quite simple. Perhaps more effectively than any other parable it illustrates the Gospel of God's redeeming love for fallen mankind.

It would be easy to regard the prodigal son of the parable as the prototype of the modern "hippie," the young "rebel without a cause," the victim of today's "drug culture." But that would be missing the point.

The prodigal son is really not hard to identify. All that we need to do is to look into our own hearts. Personal backgrounds may vary and individual experiences may differ, but essentially we must see in the prodigal son a reflection of ourselves.

Like many young people in our own affluent age, the younger son lacked for nothing that his father could give him — and yet he was not satisfied. He wanted something more: the freedom to go his own way, live his own life, without any parental restraint. At his father's expense, of course!

And so, cutting the ties of home, he struck out for "a far country." He had a gay and carefree time — while the money lasted. Stylish clothes, the choicest wines, rollicking companions made life a merry whirl.

Then disaster struck. His money ran out, a famine arose, and he suddenly found himself destitute. Yesterday's sweets turned to ashes in his mouth. Yesterday's friends somehow disappeared. Yesterday's revels were only a bitter memory.

In some way, though, he had to keep on living. There was nothing else to do than to hire himself out to a farmer for the only available job he could find—feeding the swine. Quite a comedown for our gay and free-spending young dandy!

But this menial work did not pay him enough to keep body and soul together. Even the pigs fared better than he.

Then "he came to himself." For all his folly, his degradation, his despair, he still clutched at one straw. He still had a father. More important, he was sure that his father would not turn him away if he would return, no matter how low he had sunk. Suddenly the "home place," which he had been so eager to leave, seemed the most desirable place in the world to him.

And so he decided to swallow what little pride he had left and go home. He would return not on his own terms, not to reclaim the rights of sonship, but abjectly, penitently, groveling in the dust of remorse. He would throw himself on his father's mercy, asking not to be taken back as a son but as a servant.

We all know the outcome: the father's joy, his outstretched arms, the fatted calf, the fine new clothes, the music and the laughter. Not to acclaim a returning hero-son, but to reclaim a wayward lad who had been lost but now was found!

But there is a sequel. It is supplied by the older brother— indignant, resentful, bitter. He had been faithful, decent, hard-working all his life, but no one had ever killed a fatted calf for *him!* But when the young wastrel comes back, there is a celebration that makes the rafters ring.

In a way we cannot blame the older brother. His reaction was quite human. Notice the tone of reproach: The returning ne'er-do-well is not "my brother" but "your son."

But the older brother missed the point. It is the *lost* sheep, the *lost* coin, and now the *lost* son whose recovery makes even the angels glad.

We had better not point the finger of scorn at the older brother. For in his reaction we find the reflection of our own pride, our own jealousy, our own prejudice. Not until we are ready to confess and rid ourselves of these does the Gospel's true meaning dawn on us.

To understand this parable is to understand the Gospel. The rebellious spirit, the far country, the wasted inheritance — what better description could there be of sin and its fateful consequences? The father's love, the welcome home, the boundless joy at the prodigal's return — what clearer picture of God's redeeming love, of the free forgiveness wrought by Christ, could we have?

Back from the far country to the Father's house! The way is open to all. And that way is Christ.

When Goods Are Not Good

And He told them a parable, saying, "The land of a rich man brought forth plentifully; and he thought to himself, 'What shall I do, for I have nowhere to store my crops?' And he said, 'I will do this: I will pull down my barns and build larger ones; and there I will store all my grain and my goods. And I will say to my soul, Soul, you have ample goods laid up for many years; take your ease, eat, drink, be merry.' But God said to him, 'Fool! This night your soul is required of you; and the things you have prepared, whose will they be?' So is he who lays up treasure for himself and is not rich toward God." Luke 12:16-21

For most people the term "idolatry" conjures up the picture of a squat, roly-poly Buddha, or of a tribal dance around a totem pole, or of incense burning in a heathen shrine. It is unlikely that many of us have committed that kind of idolatry. Indeed, most people in our so-called "Christian" civilization would indignantly deny that they are idolators.

And yet, we are — all of us. For "idolatry" goes far deeper than doing obeisance to a pagan idol or worshiping ancestral spirits. Idolatry is an attitude of the heart — an attitude that gives priority to material goods and values rather than to God. The object of our highest trust and affection — whatever it may be — is in fact our god. And that means shunting aside the true God, our Maker and Redeemer, who demands of all His children: "Thou shalt have no other gods before Me."

The rich fool in this parable offers a striking example of this kind of idolatry. An industrious and skillful farmer, he cultivated his land so successfully that he enjoyed bumper crops which filled his barns to overflowing.

So far, so good. There is nothing wrong in itself in being a prosperous farmer, or an astute businessman, or an affluent landholder. Material success is freighted with particular temptations. Jesus pointed out the special difficulties that beset a rich man in his effort to lead a Christian life.

The rich farmer in our parable failed the test. Instead of giving thanks to God as the source of His prosperity, he avidly grasped for more—more grain, more goods, more money, more pleasure, more ease. He congratulated himself on his own good fortune. He was sure that his wealth would provide him a safe and comfortable cushion for the years ahead.

But he was due for a rude awakening. "Fool!" God said to him. "This night your soul is required of you." Too late for the rich farmer now! Too late to remember the adage, "You can't take it with you"! For God asked him, with withering scorn: "The things you have prepared, whose will they be?"

The man in the parable was guilty of the basic sin of covetousness, or greed. And St. Paul calls the covetous man an idolator. It was idolatry—idolatry of *things*—that brought about the rich fool's downfall.

The Lord draws the inexorable conclusion: "So is he who lays up treasure for himself and is not rich toward God." In other words: Beware of making goods your god! Then goods are no longer good.

To be rich toward God is to acquire a better treasure than any the world has to offer. This is the treasure of His grace, which He offers to us in Christ. In Him we are rich indeed, both now and forever.

The Old and the New

No one puts a piece of unshrunk cloth on an old garment, for the patch tears away from the garment, and a worse tear is made. Neither is new wine put into old wineskins; if it is, the skins burst, and the wine is spilled, and the skins are destroyed; but new wine is put into fresh wineskins, and so both are preserved. Matthew 9:16-17

In our day there is a growing tendency to discard and even despise anything that is traditional, conventional, "old." The cliché "You can't trust anyone over 30" expresses the attitude of many young people. This attitude leads them to reject the wisdom, the values, the experiences of the past — even of the recent past. There is a passionate devotion to anything that is new, "different," even revolutionary.

Obviously there is both folly and danger in this indiscriminate rejection of all that is old, all that belongs to past generations. It has well been said that those who disregard the lessons of history are doomed to repeat them. This is manifestly true in the matter of moral and spiritual values.

In another sense, however, the Christian religion demands a complete break with the past. It presents us with something totally new — new values, new goals, a new life. "Behold, I make all things new," says our Lord. And St. Paul declares that "if anyone is in Christ, he is a new creation; the old has passed away, behold, the new has come."

This is the lesson that Jesus meant to teach in these two related parables. If a new piece of cloth is sewed on an old garment, the patch will make the garment tear. If new wine is poured into an old wineskin, the wineskin will break.

The spiritual application is clear. The Gospel of Christ has brought something new into the world: new love, new hope, new freedom, new trust in the gracious promises of God, new strength to live in obedience to His will.

It is both foolish and fatal to try to press the new life in Christ into the old, legalistic mold of work righteousness, to hem in the new freedom of the Gospel with a high wall of commands and prohibitions, to cast over God's "new creation" the shadow of old laws, old rituals, old traditions.

Old cloth and old wineskins—these are the symbols of the Old Covenant that came to an end with the coming of Christ. His life and death and resurrection ushered in the New Covenant of grace. Now all who accept Him as Lord and Savior are clothed with the new garment of His righteousness; they drink the new wine of spiritual liberty. And someday they will sing the new song of eternal joy and praise before the throne of God.

To Forgive Is Divine

Therefore the kingdom of heaven may be compared to a king who wished to settle accounts with his servants. When he began the reckoning, one was brought to him who owed him ten thousand talents; and as he could not pay, his lord ordered him to be sold, with his wife and children and all that he had, and payment to be made. So the servant fell on his knees, imploring him, "Lord, have patience with me, and I will pay you everything." And out of pity for him the lord of that servant released him and forgave him the debt. But that same servant, as he went out, came upon one of his fellow servants who owed him a hundred denarii; and seizing him by the throat he said, "Pay what you owe." So his fellow servant fell down and besought him, "Have patience with me, and I will pay you." He refused and went and put him in prison till he should pay the debt. When his fellow servants saw what had taken place, they were greatly distressed, and they went and reported to their lord all that had taken place. Then his lord summoned him and said to him, "You wicked servant! I forgave you all that debt because you besought me; and should not you have had mercy on your fellow servant, as I had mercy on you?" And in anger his lord delivered him to the jailers, till he should pay all his debt. So also My heavenly Father will do to every one of you, if you do not forgive your brother from your heart. Matthew 18:23-35

The current indebtedness of the United States is now inching up toward four hundred billion dollars—a sum so enormous that we are inclined to say, "Such an incredible amount of money—how can it ever be repaid?"

The first servant in our parable must have felt that way about the staggering debt that he had incurred. Even in this era of inflated currency, his debt might amount to some ten million dollars. We need not quibble about the question of whether any servant could ever get that deeply into debt with his master. The hyperbole simply emphasizes the fact that the debt was so great that it could never possibly be repaid.

This fact underscores the generosity of the king in writing off the debt and in revoking the harsh sentence that he had imposed upon the debtor and his family. Jesus says, "Out of pity for him the lord of that servant released him and forgave him the debt."

The lesson, of course, is obvious. The king is the Lord Himself. The servant represents each one of us. The debt that we owe to Him is no monetary sum or any material obligation. The debt consists in our sin and guilt, our pride and unbelief. No human exertion, no sacrificial offerings can even begin to repay our debt to God. That is why we plead in the Lord's Prayer: "Forgive us our debts."

There is only one way to clear our account. That is the grace of God. Like the king in the parable, the Lord has had pity upon us. And what pity! An act of divine generosity incomparably greater than even the cancellation of a debt of ten million dollars!

But that is only half the story. The servant whose enormous debt had just been forgiven apparently learned nothing from the example of his generous master. For when he encountered one of his fellow servants who owed him the trivial sum of a hundred denarii—about twenty dollars—he grabbed him by the throat and demanded immediate payment.

Of no avail were the hapless servant's pleas for a grace period. "Have patience with me, and I will pay you," he begged. But the first servant turned a deaf ear. "To the debtor's prison!" was his harsh reply.

When word of this episode reached the master's ear, he was incensed. His reaction was quick and decisive. Without further ado the jail doors soon clanged behind the hardhearted servant.

"To forgive is divine," the saying goes. That divine quality must be reflected also in the Christian attitude toward those who have grieved and offended us. Even the greatest debt that is owed us is small indeed when compared with the incalculable debt that we owe to God—and that He has already canceled.

But there is perhaps nothing harder for us to do than to forgive those who have injured us and caused us heartache. The natural thing is to bear a grudge, to harbor resentment, to withhold the hand of forgiveness.

Just because this is the "natural" reaction, forgiveness appears as truly a divine quality. It is a divine gift to be able to overcome our natural resentment and to say those difficult but deeply and essentially Christian words, "I forgive."

To forgive the wrongdoer brings relief to him, to be sure. But to forgive brings even greater blessing to the one who does the forgiving. It is a cleansing, strengthening, ennobling experience.

Yes, more: It is a "divine" experience. For to forgive is to express the spirit of that love which is God's own gift. That love, indeed, belongs to the very nature of God.

That experience can be—must be—ours.

The Seed and the Weeds

The kingdom of heaven may be compared to a man who sowed good seed in his field; but while men were sleeping, his enemy came and sowed weeds among the wheat, and went away. So when the plants came up and bore grain, then the weeds appeared also. And the servants of the householder came and said to him, "Sir, did you not sow good seed in your field? How then has it weeds?" He said to them, "An enemy has done this." The servants said to him, "Then do you want us to go and gather them?" But he said, "No; lest in gathering the weeds you root up the wheat along with them. Let both grow together until the harvest; and at harvest time I will tell the reapers, Gather the weeds first and bind them in bundles to be burned, but gather the wheat into my barn."
Matthew 13:24-30

His disciples came to him, saying, "Explain to us the parable of the weeds in the field." He answered, "He who sows the good seed is the Son of Man; the field is the world, and the good seed means the sons of the kingdom; the weeds are the sons of the Evil One, and the enemy who sowed them is the devil; the harvest is the close of the age, and the reapers are angels. Just as the weeds are gathered and burned with fire, so it will be at the close of the age. The Son of Man will send His angels, and they will gather out of His kingdom all causes of sin and all evildoers, and throw them into the furnace of fire; there men will weep and gnash their teeth. Then the righteous will shine like the sun in the kingdom of their Father." Matthew 13:36-43

This is another of Jesus' agricultural parables, reflecting the experiences and interests of His hearers in largely rural Palestine. The lesson, however, is of universal and enduring significance. It presents an especially apt allegory of God's kingdom.

Every farmer knows about weeds—what a nuisance they are,

what economic loss they entail. No farmer in his right mind would sow "tares among the wheat." But they appear nevertheless. To the harried, weed-plagued farmer it must indeed seem that "an enemy has done this"—at least some hostile force within nature.

The spiritual application is made clear by Jesus. The good seed of God's Word is sown far and wide. Wherever the Gospel is preached, there faith is created, new life is engendered, souls are brought into the kingdom.

Inevitably, however, wherever the good seed is sown, weeds also crop up. Along with the true believers, there are bound to be those who are Christians in name only—hypocritical, shallow, self-serving in their apparent acceptance of the Word. In Dietrich Bonhoeffer's phrase, they regard grace as "cheap" rather than free. They see in God's proffer of forgiveness an open invitation to continue their old selfish ways, to indulge their own pride and peccadilloes, confident that their passport to heaven is secure.

Who are these people, these weeds in God's field? The answer to this question is perhaps the most important—and most easily overlooked—lesson in this parable.

The identification of these spiritual "weeds" must be God's judgment, not our own. This goes counter to our natural inclinations. Like the servants in the parable, we want to proceed forthwith to root out the weeds and cast them into the fire.

Virtue is good—but virtue can be arrogant. It can be too hasty in pointing the finger of scorn at the wrongdoer, in wanting to "write him off" as an incorrigible sinner. "Expunge, expel, excommunicate!" cries Virtue as she draws up her skirts in Pharisaical pride to avoid the contamination of the world. Sanctimonious moralism too often appears as a caricature of genuine Christian virtue.

Orthodoxy is good, but orthodoxy can be arrogant, too. Concern for so-called "pure doctrine" has often led to the most

61

insidious kind of spiritual pride. Too often we are ready to consign to outer darkness anyone whose profession of the faith does not conform, in minutest detail, to our own understanding of Holy Scripture. Such people, we declaim, should leave the church, and if they don't do so willingly, we are quite ready to hasten their exit. "Heretic, rebel, a thing to flout!" is the cry of outraged orthodoxy.

Now, we do not intend to minimize the importance of either personal virtue or doctrinal integrity. Christian love does not mean indifference to sin and its causes. Departures from God's standards, in both faith and life, must indeed come under judgment.

But this must be *God's* judgment, not personal prejudice. And such judgment must await the final confirmation of the Last Day. Then the Lord Himself will cause His angel-reapers to separate the weeds from the wheat and will announce His just and final verdict.

Meanwhile, we cultivate the good seed that the Son of Man keeps sowing through the preaching of the Word—in the world and in our own life. For by His grace we hope at last to be joined to "the righteous," who "will shine like the sun in the kingdom of the Father."

Counting the Cost

Now great multitudes accompanied Him; and He turned and said to them, "If anyone comes to Me and does not hate his own father and mother and wife and children and brothers and sisters, yes, and even his own life, he cannot be My disciple. Whoever does not bear his own cross and come after Me, cannot be My disciple. For which of you, desiring to build a tower, does not first sit down and count the cost, whether he has enough to complete it? Otherwise, when he has laid a foundation and is not able to finish, all who see it begin to mock him, saying, 'This man began to build, and was not able to finish.' Or what king, going to encounter another king in war, will not sit down first and take counsel whether he is able with ten thousand to meet him who comes against him with twenty thousand? And if not, while the other is yet a great way off, he sends an embassy and asks terms of peace. So therefore, whoever of you does not renounce all that he has cannot be My disciple." Luke 14:25-33

These two brief parables are among the most difficult of any that Jesus told—difficult in the apparently harsh and unyielding demands that Jesus places upon His followers. A young man of our acquaintance rejected Christianity because of the words by which Jesus introduced this particular lesson. He had no use, he argued, for a religion that demands hatred of one's own parents and family.

The young man, of course, completely misunderstood the spirit of Jesus' words and took them out of their context. For one thing, the word which is here translated "hate" in the original Greek actually means to "love less." What is more, the whole thrust of Jesus' lesson is that discipleship requires a radical break with everything that might detract from our complete allegiance to Him. Membership in God's kingdom requires *total* commitment.

No halfhearted service, no divided loyalties, no nostalgia for our past, Christless way of life can be tolerated. Even the nearest and most beloved of our kith and kin cannot claim a higher place in our love than Christ, nor can they interfere with our service to Him.

Jesus drives home this lesson with two parables: the cost of building a tower, and the cost of going to war. It takes a foolish builder not to determine beforehand the probable cost of his project. For example, in the Indonesian capital city of Djakarta there are a number of tall buildings—empty and unfinished—commissioned by the late dictator, Sukarno. The money ran out before they could be completed. So they stand there like gaunt skeletons, monuments to one man's folly in not "counting the cost."

The history of military warfare likewise bears ample and bloody testimony to the lesson of the second parable. Germany and Japan lost World War II because their military leaders did not count the cost of engaging a superior foe—and so they brought disaster upon their beautiful countries and upon their courageous people.

Nothing looks more bleak than an unfinished tower, or more wretched than a defeated army. The tragedy is compounded when these failures could have been avoided through sound and cautious planning.

This truism, of course, is infinitely sadder in the spiritual realm. We all can think of examples of eager young people, fired with zeal for Christ on their confirmation day, whose spiritual ardor began to cool when they went out to face the world. Their tower cost more than they expected; the opposing armies were too strong for them. They were just not ready for the radical demands that their Christian calling placed upon them.

Every overseas missionary can recount sad tales of converts

from Buddhism or Hinduism or some other religion — or from no religion at all — who embraced their newfound Christian faith with passionate zeal. But then the flame began to flicker under the opposition of family members, the pressure of social and business associates, or the beckoning allurements of the world. Every mission field is littered with the skeletons of unfinished towers and with the debris of lost battles.

And so Jesus concludes, "So therefore, whoever of you does not renounce all that he has cannot be My disciple." Our Lord does not counsel a hermit existence. He does counsel a life of total commitment to Him. He does demand *number one* priority in our lives for Him, His kingdom, His righteousness.

Then all of our other loves and loyalties will fall into their proper places. The unworthy ones will be sloughed off, while those that are worthy will be sanctified by our supreme love and loyalty to Him.

That means counting the cost. And we shall find the cost worthwhile.

Hidden Treasure

The kingdom of heaven is like treasure hidden in a field, which a man found and covered up; then in his joy he goes and sells all that he has and buys that field. Again, the kingdom of heaven is like a merchant in search of fine pearls, who, on finding one pearl of great value, went and sold all that he had and bought it. Matthew 13:44-46

Life is a never-ending quest. Men seek what to them appears to be the highest good—love, wealth, happiness, fame, health, security. When a man stops seeking, he is ready to die.

Everything depends, however, on the object of our quest. Rather, all depends upon the priorities that we assign to the various goals that we seek to attain as we make our way through life. Too often, when the goal is achieved and the treasure is found, it crumbles to dust in our grasp. Right goals and right priorities are all-important if our quest is to be successful—and blessed.

Our Lord illustrates this truth in this pair of short and simple parables, which both teach the same lesson. In the first the prospector found his sought-for treasure hidden in a field. In the second the pearl merchant discovered one pearl which transcended all the others in value.

In both cases the finders promptly sold all that they had in order to acquire the immensely valuable object of their quest. No sacrifice was too great to keep them from their goal. Obviously they regarded their investment as supremely worthwhile. There was no question as to their priorities.

The point of both parables, of course, is that the kingdom of heaven is the hidden treasure and the pearl of great value. It must receive the highest priority in our life. It must be the supreme object of our quest. To find it and to keep it as our own is worth all manner of sacrifice.

We are too often loath, however, to "sell all that we have." We yearn so much to cling to some of life's gaudy but empty baubles, to keep tasting its luscious but forbidden fruit, to tuck away some of the world's glittering but worthless coin in some hidden pocket of our lives. We are not quite willing to give God's kingdom the top priority that He demands, and to "sell all that we have" to obtain it.

A pastor once told us of a community canvass conducted by the members of his parish. When one canvasser met the objection, "Oh, you have to give up too much when you join a church!" his reply was, "Oh, no, you don't have to give up anything in *our* church!"

But our Lord teaches that for the Kingdom's sake the Christian must give up everything—everything that takes precedence over God. We must "sell all that we have" to buy the field with the buried treasure, to buy the pearl of great price.

Actually, what the Christian must "sell"—or renounce—is himself, his pride, his ego, his self-love. The price is high, but the gain is great.

What is the world to me, with all its vaunted pleasure,
When Thou, and Thou alone, Lord Jesus, art my Treasure!

Proper Dress

And again Jesus spoke to them in parables, saying, "The kingdom of heaven may be compared to a king who gave a marriage feast for his son, and sent his servants to call those who were invited to the marriage feast; but they would not come. Again he sent other servants, saying, 'Tell those who are invited, Behold, I have made ready my dinner, my oxen and my fat calves are killed, and everything is ready; come to the marriage feast.' But they made light of it and went off, one to his farm, another to his business, while the rest seized his servants, treated them shamefully, and killed them. The king was angry, and he sent his troops and destroyed those murderers and burned their city. Then he said to his servants, 'The wedding is ready, but those invited were not worthy. Go therefore to the thoroughfares, and invite to the marriage feast as many as you find.' And those servants went out into the streets and gathered all whom they found, both bad and good; so the wedding hall was filled with guests. But when the king came in to look at the guests, he saw there a man who had no wedding garment; and he said to him, 'Friend, how did you get in here without a wedding garment?' And he was speechless. Then the king said to the attendants, 'Bind him hand and foot, and cast him into the outer darkness; there men will weep and gnash their teeth.' For many are called, but few are chosen." Matthew 22:1-14

Styles of dress, for both men and women, have been changing markedly in recent times. Indeed, sometimes it is difficult to tell the sexes apart. Often we hear the comment, "It's not what a man wears on the outside but what he is on the inside that is really important."

There is an element of truth in this statement. Nevertheless, a man's style of dress often gives some indication of his personality and his inner attitudes. A pastor who would make his hospital calls dressed like a racetrack tout, or a banker who would receive prospective investors wearing shoulder-length hair and hippie-style love beads, or a doctor who would call on his patients in a greasy sweat shirt and dungarees would inspire little confidence. There is nothing essentially immoral about such attire, but it would reveal a nonprofessional attitude, to say the least. Clothes do not "make the man," but they do tell something about the man.

Our Lord has something to say about proper attire in this parable. The kind of garment that he is concerned about, however, is not material but spiritual. And therein lies a lesson for us all.

It was the custom in Biblical times for wedding guests to attend the festivities in a special type of robe. In fact, this garment was in effect a badge of admission to the ceremony.

The parable tells of a marriage feast which a king gave in honor of his son. To his chagrin his invitations were insultingly, even violently, rejected. The king then had his servants scour the streets and lanes of the city and invite all of those whom they found, "both bad and good." In this way, at least, the wedding hall was filled.

Presumably all the guests appeared in the conventional wedding garment — all, that is, but one. When he could offer no good excuse for his neglect of proper attire, the king had him thrown out.

The wedding feast, of course, represents God's kingdom. The invitation goes out to all. Many, unfortunately, reject it. They are too busy, too indifferent, too contemptuous of the divine offer. Although many are called, few accept.

These few are the "chosen," says Jesus. They could not get to the wedding on their own initiative, or relying on their own resources, or on the basis of their own merits. The king's invitation, and their appearance at the feast, is a matter of pure grace.

To be admitted to the wedding hall, of course, they must appear in the proper garment. This garment is the righteousness of Christ, which is put on through repentance and faith — faith in the love and mercy of the divine Host, and in the redemption provided by the atoning merits of His Son.

It is not sufficient for the invited guests just to brush off or to patch up the old garment that they may be wearing. The robe in which they are to appear at the wedding must be completely new, clean, spotlessly white.

We cannot present ourselves at the divine marriage feast wearing the garment of our own righteousness, our own morality, our trust in "cheap grace." Such a garment will not gain admission for us even though we adorn it with some Christian embellishments and symbols. The garment that seems beautiful to us is nothing but a "filthy rag," as Isaiah puts it, in the sight of God. We must strip it off and bedeck ourselves in the bright and shining "wedding garment" which His grace alone can provide.

This alone is "proper dress" in which to appear before the King.

Jesus, Thy blood and righteousness
My beauty are, my glorious dress.

Have We Enough Oil?

Then the kingdom of heaven shall be compared to ten maidens who took their lamps and went to meet the bridegroom. Five of them were foolish, and five were wise. For when the foolish took their lamps, they took no oil with them; but the wise took flasks of oil with their lamps. As the bridegroom was delayed, they all slumbered and slept. But at midnight there was a cry, "Behold, the bridegroom! Come out to meet him." Then all those maidens rose and trimmed their lamps. And the foolish said to the wise, "Give us some of your oil, for our lamps are going out." But the wise replied, "Perhaps there will not be enough for us and for you; go rather to the dealers and buy for yourselves." And while they went to buy, the bridegroom came, and those who were ready went in with him to the marriage feast; and the door was shut. Afterward the other maidens came also, saying, "Lord, lord, open to us." But he replied, "Truly, I say to you, I do not know you." Watch therefore, for you know neither the day nor the hour. Matthew 25:1-13

Along the highways of America one sometimes sees a sign erected by some religious group, reading: "Prepare to meet thy God!" We have seen the sign so often that we tend to ignore it. Some motorists even jest about it. But the sign, for all its crudeness, does convey an important truth. Sooner or later we are all going to meet our God. And so we had better prepare ourselves to meet Him when He comes—whether at the end of the world or at the end of our own lives.

We know two things about the Second Coming of our Lord. The first is, of course, that His coming is a certainty. The second is that the exact time of His coming is a mystery. Putting these two facts together should lead to the obvious conclusion that we ought to be ready for Him at any time.

It should be obvious, but to many people it evidently is not.

They act as though the Lord will never come. Then, when His arrival is announced, they are not prepared to meet Him. But by that time it is too late.

This is the simple, central lesson of this parable. But the behavior of the two groups of maidens may warrant a bit closer scrutiny.

All ten of the girls had been informed of the imminent coming of the bridegroom. The difference was that the first group awaited His coming well-prepared. To make sure that they would not miss him, they took plenty of extra oil for their lamps. They left nothing to chance. They were even confident enough to catch some sleep while they were waiting.

The other five, however, were literally "caught napping." When the midnight herald called, they found to their dismay that their supply of oil had run out. There was no time to buy, beg, or borrow any more. And so the bridegroom's coming found them unprepared. All their plaintive cries, all their frantic pounding on the door did not gain them entry to the marriage feast.

Were they treated too harshly? Not really. Not when we consider the fact that the girls had plenty of warning of his coming, plenty of time to prepare. They had even been supplied with the necessary equipment. All they needed was oil—and the foresight to lay in a supply beforehand. But they were too lazy, too indifferent, or too shortsighted. And so they missed out on the festivities.

God has supplied us with the lamp of His Word. But the lamp will not give us any light without the oil that the Holy Spirit supplies. That oil is faith. It is not enough simply to have the lamp on hand. We must fill the lamp with oil and keep it burning.

When the Bridegroom comes, the question will not merely be, "Do you have a lamp?" but "Is your lamp filled with oil, and is it burning?" It is not enough to have a Bible on our shelf.

We must have genuine faith in the saving teachings of God's Word. We must accept in our hearts the Gospel of God's love in Christ. And then we must exhibit our faith in a life of love, service, action. For the lamp is not to burn only for our own benefit, but also to give light to those around us.

With lamps aglow, we shall be ready to meet the Bridegroom when He comes—and to light the way for others too.